Editors
Karen Tam Froloff
Gisela Lee

Editorial Manager
Karen J. Goldfluss, M.S. Ed.

Editor-in-Chief
Sharon Coan, M.S. Ed.

Cover Artist
Jessica Orlando

Art Coordinator
Denice Adorno

Imaging
Rosa C. See

Product Manager
Phil Garcia

Publishers
Rachelle Cracchiolo, M.S. Ed.
Mary Dupuy Smith, M.S. Ed.

How to Work Probability and Statistics

Grades 6–8

Author

Robert W. Smith

Teacher Created Materials, Inc.
6421 Industry Way
Westminster, CA 92683
www.teachercreated.com
ISBN-1-57690-968-9
©2002 Teacher Created Materials, Inc.
Made in U.S.A.

Table of Contents

A Note to Teachers and Parents

Welcome to the "How to" math series! You have chosen one of over two dozen books designed to give your children the information and practice they need to acquire important concepts in specific areas of math. The goal of the "How to" math books is to give children an extra boost as they work toward mastery of the math skills established by the National Council of Teachers of Mathematics (NCTM) and ordained in grade-level scope and sequence guidelines.

The design of this book is intended to be used by teachers or parents for a variety of purposes and needs. Each of the units contains one "How to" page and two or more practice pages. The "How to" section of each unit precedes the practice pages and provides needed information such as a concept or math rule to review, important terms and formulas to remember, or step-by-step guidelines necessary for using the practice pages.

About This Book

How to Work with Probability and Statistics: Grades 6–8 presents a comprehensive overview of strategies for working with data, statistics, tables, graphs and visuals of all kinds, the measures of central tendency, theoretical and experimental probability, and related word problems. The units include clear, simple, and readable instruction pages and student activities. This book, therefore, can be used as an instruction vehicle for introducing and teaching statistics and probability to students with little or no background in the concepts.

The units in this book can be used in whole-class instruction with the teacher or by a parent assisting his or her child through the book.

This book also lends itself to use by a small group doing remedial work on probability and statistics or individuals and small groups in earlier grades engaged in enrichment or advanced work. A teacher may want to have two tracks within her class with one moving at a faster pace and the other at a gradual pace appropriate to the ability or background of her students. The units in this book can also be used in a learning center with materials specified for each unit of instruction.

Teachers and parents working with children who are new to the various concepts in this book should take more time reviewing the "How to" pages with the children. Students should also be allowed to use the calculator to check the accuracy of their work, where appropriate. This reduces the need for correction and allows the material to be self-corrected, if desired.

If students have difficulty on a specific concept or unit within this book, review the material and allow them to redo the troublesome pages. Since concept development is sequential, it is not advisable to skip much of the material in the book. It is preferable that children find the work easy and gradually advance to the more difficult concepts.

Encourage students to use manipulatives, such as coins, dice, and spinners, to reinforce the concepts. They should use tally sheets, tables, and graphs as well as other visual materials to reinforce the concepts and encourage full mastery of the material.

How to Work with Probability and Statistics: Grades 6-8 matches a number of NCTM standards, including these main topics and specific features:

Statistics

This book highlights the NCTM standard that students should have diverse and extensive experiences with organizing, collecting, and representing data. They should become proficient in representing data on a wide variety of tables, graphs, and other visual expressions. Students need to recognize the value of data, understand when it is used in misleading ways, and be able to analyze raw data in meaningful and useable ways. They should ultimately be able to use statistical analysis as a method of mathematical and real-life decision making.

Probability

The NCTM standard that students should have many experiences with both theoretical and experimental probability is highlighted. Students should be able to apply probability models to data and make predictions based on both theoretical and experimental expressions of probability. They should recognize the wide range of probability applications in the real world.

Mathematics as Problem Solving

Expressed in this book is a strong commitment that the study of mathematics should emphasize problem solving in such a way that students can use problem-solving approaches to investigate and understand the general content of mathematics. Students are encouraged to solve problems involving everyday situations and real-life applications of math skills, especially as they relate to probability and statistics.

Computation and Estimation

The problems in this book strongly encourage the learning of the four basic operations and other processes in the context of data analysis, probability models, problem-solving experiences, and real-world applications. They develop aptitude and confidence in students' computational ability and their ability to apply mathematics meaningfully.

Communication

Students are given numerous opportunities to apply physical diagrams, charts, graphs, tables, tally sheets, pictures, and materials to concrete mathematical ideas. Students can relate their everyday common language to the expression of mathematical ideas and symbols on a level appropriate to their age. Students will also understand that mathematics involves discussion, reading, writing, and listening as integral functions of mathematical instruction.

Reasoning

Students learn to apply logic to their math problems and to justify their answers. There is an emphasis on the use of models, manipulatives, and charts. Students learn to apply rational thinking effectively and correctly to problems rooted in real-life circumstances.

Connections

Students are encouraged to recognize and relate various mathematical concepts, processes, and patterns to each other. They are likewise encouraged to use mathematics across the curriculum and in their daily lives.

Facts to Know

- **Statistics** is that aspect of math, which involves the collection, organization, display, and analysis of data.
- **Data** is a set of individual pieces of information, usually in numerical form.
- **Raw data** is a collection of individual units of information before they have been organized or arranged.
- **Frequency** refers to the number of times a specific piece of data was found.

Data needs to be organized into groups according to some particular guidelines or arranged in a specific order, such as from least to greatest.

Tables

Raw data can be organized or arranged in tables, which record the frequency with which an event occurred, or the number of units for each category.

Raw Data and Tables

Sixth Graders' Favorite TV Programming

Sample A (Raw Data)

A survey of 33 sixth graders' favorite type of TV shows was recorded on this tally sheet.

Tally Sheet	
Sports	ЖΗ III
Drama	I
Sitcoms	ЖΗ ЖΗ II
Movies	III
Nature/Science	I
Science Fiction	II
Wrestling	IIII
Other	II

Sample B (Table)

The tally sheet from Sample A is now arranged in table format.

Program Type	Frequency
Sports	8
Drama	1
Sitcoms	12
Movies	3
Nature/Science	1
Science Fiction	2
Wrestling	4
Other	2

Graphs

Data can be visually represented or displayed on graphs.

Sample C (Bar Graph)

This bar graph offers an effective visual display of the data collected in Sample A and organized in Sample B.

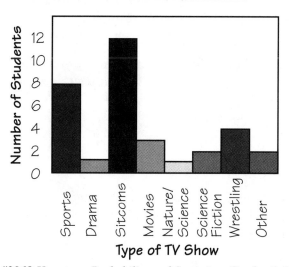

Directions: Use the information on page 5 to help you organize the data on this page.

1. The record sheet below shows the results of a study of 20 ladybugs with the number of dots on the outer wings of each ladybug recorded.

Record Sheet for Ladybug Dots

(9, 13, 0, 13, 11, 9, 0, 13, 13, 7, 2, 13, 9, 7, 2, 13, 9, 14, 13, 13)

Complete this frequency table for Ladybug Dots using the information from the record sheet.

Dots	0	1	2	3	4	5	6	7	8	9	10	11	12	13	14
Frequency															

2. Teresa looked all over the house for loose change. She checked under sofas, on the floor, in drawers, and in similar places. Look at her tally sheet below. Then use the table on the right to organize her data.

Tally Sheet of Loose Coins	
Pennies	ЖЖ ЖЖ ЖЖ ЖЖ III
Nickels	ЖЖ IIII
Dimes	ЖЖ ЖЖ ЖЖ
Quarters	IIII
Half-dollars	

Table of Loose Coins	Frequency
Pennies	
Nickels	
Dimes	
Quarters	
Half-dollars	

Extension

- Make a survey of all of the students in your class to determine their favorite television programming. Use the survey included here. Add other types of programming if you wish.

- After you have completed the tally sheet, complete a frequency table like the one on page 5 to organize your results.

- Create a tally sheet to survey your classmates on their favorite sports to watch or play. Then complete a frequency table to record your findings.

Tally Sheet	
Sports	
Drama	
Sitcoms	
Movies	
Nature/Science	
Science Fiction	
Wrestling	
Other	

Directions: Use the information on page 5 to organize the raw data from these tally sheets into tables or charts. Then answer the questions related to each set of data.

Number of Medals Awarded at Arrow Valley School "Olympics Day"

	sprints	relay	long jump	sit-ups	pull-ups
6th grade boys	Ж	II	III	III	II
6th grade girls	IIII	III	III	II	I
7th grade boys	Ж I	IIII	Ж	IIII	IIII
7th grade girls	Ж	Ж I	IIII	III	III
8th grade boys	III	III	II	Ж	III
8th grade girls	IIII	II	II	II	II

1. Make a table to organize the data on the tally sheet.

2. Which of the six groups won the most medals? _____

3. Which of the three classes was probably the most athletic? _____

4. Which of the five activities was probably the hardest? _____

5. How many medals did the boys win? _____

6. How many medals did the girls win? _____

Numbers Generated Rolling Two Dice 24 Times

2	3	4	5	6	7	8	9	10	11	12
I	Ø	I	III	IIII	Ж	III	III	II	I	I

7. Make a table to organize the above data.

8. Which number had no rolls? _____

9. Which four numbers combined had the same number of rolls as 6? _____ _____ _____ _____

10. Which numbers were rolled the most often? _____ Why do you think this happened?

_____

Extension

- Roll two dice 24 times. Keep a tally sheet to record each roll.

- Make a table to organize your data.

- Compare your results to the data on this page.

- Compare your table with those of your classmates.

- Create a combined table showing the results for 10 members of your class. (Include yourself.)

Directions: Use the information on page 5 to help you do this page.

This is a tally sheet indicating the number of absences during one week for 7th grade students in each homeroom.

7th Grade Arrow Valley Middle School Weekly Absence Report

	Monday	Tuesday	Wednesday	Thursday	Friday
Room 12	III	II	I	II	IIII
Room 13	ЖⅠ	III	II	III	ЖⅠ Ⅰ
Room 14	II	I			II
Room 15	III	III	I		I
Room 16	I	I	I	I	III
Room 17	II			III	II
Room 18	IIII	I		I	IIII

1. Create a table to organize this data both by day and by weekly totals.

2. What were the total absences for the week in the 7th grade? _____

3. Which homeroom had the fewest absences? _____

4. Which day of the week had the best attendance? _____

5. Which two days had the worst attendance? _____

6. Give a possible reason for the poor attendance on these days. _____

   _____

7. How many students were absent on Tuesday? _____

8. Which room had the worst attendance? _____

9. Two students were absent the entire week in room 13. How many other absences did room 13 have? _____

10. Could any one else have been absent the entire week in any room? Explain. _____

    _____

Apple Valley Middle School has a snack table after school, which helps raise money for school projects. This tally sheet illustrates their sales for one afternoon.

11. Create a table to organize this data.

12. Which product was the best seller?

    _____

13. Which two products were the least popular? _____

14. Did the students mainly buy healthy snacks or sweets? _____

15. How many snacks were sold altogether? _____

16. If every snack sold for $0.50, how much money was collected? _____

Snack Table Sales for Thursday

apples	II
juice	ЖⅠ Ⅰ
colas	ЖⅠ ЖⅠ ЖⅠ ЖⅠ ЖⅠ ЖⅠ Ⅰ
candy bars	ЖⅠ ЖⅠ ЖⅠ ЖⅠ ЖⅠ ЖⅠ III
chips	ЖⅠ ЖⅠ ЖⅠ ЖⅠ IIII
peanuts	ЖⅠ II
raisins	III
candy jellies	ЖⅠ ЖⅠ ЖⅠ ЖⅠ ЖⅠ ЖⅠ ЖⅠ

How to Use and Interpret Bar, Circle, and Line Graphs

Facts to Know

Graphs are effective tools used to compare data in clear, concise, visual terms.

Three of the most common graphs are bar graphs, circle graphs (pie charts), and line graphs.

Graphing Terms

- The **range** is the difference between the least and the greatest values in a set of data.

  (2, 4, 7, 8, 10, 12)

  12 – 2 = 10

  The *range* is 10.

- The **scale** is the set of values or numbers along the side of a graph.

- The **interval** is the regular difference between each unit on the scale. The interval is always the same between each unit of the scale.

- The **axes** are the two labeled lines, one vertical and one horizontal, along the sides of a graph. The scale runs along one of the axes.

Single Bar Graphs

Single bar graphs offer a clear, visual presentation of facts. Bar graphs may be either vertical or horizontal. The names of the items being compared are listed, one in each block, along the bottom axis of the bar graph. The scale is marked in even intervals along the vertical axis.

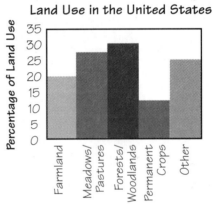

Land Use in the United States

Single Line Graphs

Single line graphs are often used to compare change over time or the frequency of an event. The time intervals or items being compared are marked along the horizontal axis of the line graph. The scale is marked in even intervals along the vertical axis.

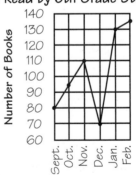

Books Read by 6th Grade Students

Circle Graphs (Pie Charts)

Circle graphs, or *pie charts*, demonstrate how a whole is split into individual parts.

The parts are rarely equal. The size of the angle shows how one part compares to another. They are usually expressed in percentages of the whole, based on 100%. Labels, listing names and amounts, are written on the slices of the graph.

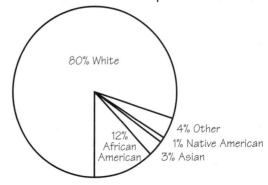

Racial Distribution in U.S. Population

This single bar graph shows the number of electoral votes for each of the 10 most populated states. The states are labeled in blocks along the horizontal axis. The number of electoral votes is indicated on the vertical axis. There are 538 electoral votes distributed among the 50 states and the District of Columbia. They are elected by the people in each state to officially vote for the president of the United States. It takes 270 electoral votes to win an election.

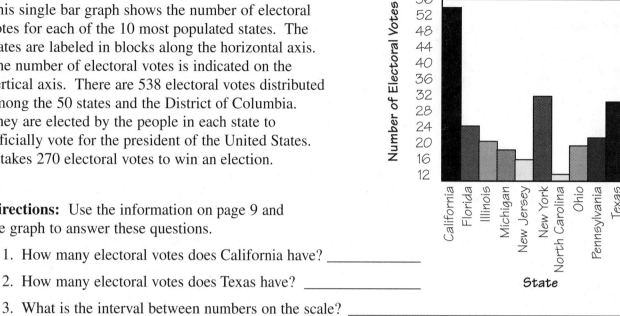

Directions: Use the information on page 9 and the graph to answer these questions.

1. How many electoral votes does California have? _____

2. How many electoral votes does Texas have? _____

3. What is the interval between numbers on the scale? _____

4. How many electoral votes does New Jersey have?_____

5. What is the difference in the number of votes between Michigan and Illinois? _____

6. Which state has exactly one more electoral vote than Texas? _____

7. What is the total number of electoral votes of the 10 most populated states? _____

8. How many electoral votes are distributed among the remaining 40 states and the District of Columbia? _____

9. Why would a candidate spend more time campaigning in California than in North Carolina?

    _____

10. How many more votes than these 10 states would be needed to win a presidential election?

    _____

11. Which two pairs of states have the same number of electoral votes as California?

    _____

12. Why did the intervals start with 12 votes? _____

13. What could be misleading about this graph? _____

Extension

Ten students at Arrow Valley Middle School were surveyed to determine the number of times they went to a fast food restaurant in one week. This table shows the results. Use the information to create a single bar graph.

Number of Fast Food Visits in One Week

Name	Frequency	Name	Frequency
John	3	Freddy	5
Sherry	6	Elaine	1
Jimmy	10	Ginette	4
Alex	0	Harry	3
Marianne	2	Hector	7

This circle graph illustrates which elements are most abundant in the earth's crust.

Directions: Use the information on page 9 and the circle graph to answer these questions.

1. Which is the most abundant element in the earth's crust? _____

2. Which two elements make up three-fourth's of the earth's crust? _____
_____

3. Which two elements together are equal to the amount of aluminum in the earth's crust?
_____

4. Where would carbon, hydrogen, and sodium be included?_____

5. Which element makes up almost half of the earth's crust? _____

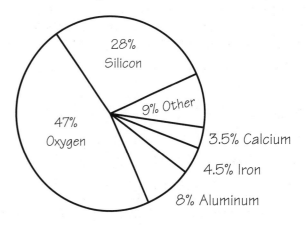

Elements as a Percentage of the Earth's Crust

28% Silicon
9% Other
47% Oxygen
3.5% Calcium
4.5% Iron
8% Aluminum

This circle graph illustrates the percentages of each major element in the human body.

6. Which element makes up more than half of the human body? _____

7. How much higher is the percentage of carbon than the percentage of nitrogen? _____

8. What percentage of the human body do the three major elements total? _____

9. On the graph, where do you think copper, phosphorus, and iron are included?
_____

10. What body compound would have much of the hydrogen and oxygen?_____

11. Why is this type of graph so easy to use?
_____
_____
_____

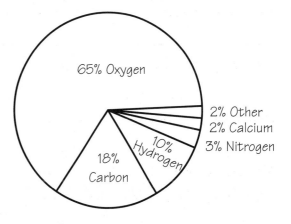

Major Elements as a Percentage of the Human Body

65% Oxygen
2% Other
2% Calcium
10% Hydrogen
3% Nitrogen
18% Carbon

Extension

- Survey 10 members of your class to determine their favorite pizza topping. Convert each topping to a percentage. (If three of the ten students prefer pepperoni, that is 30% of the total. If one student prefers cheese, that is 10% of the total.)
- Create a circle graph illustrating the results of your survey.

The two line graphs indicate the number of hours spent on homework for two 8th grade students.

Number of Hours Spent on Homework in One Week

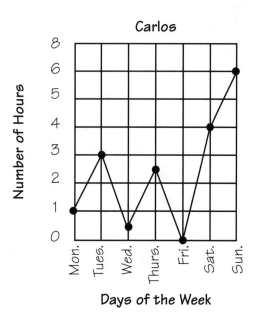

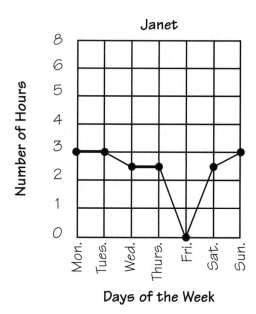

Directions: Use the information on page 9 and the two graphs above to answer these questions.

1. How many hours did Carlos spend doing homework on Tuesday? _____

2. How many hours did Janet spend doing homework on Tuesday? _____

3. On which day did neither student do any homework? _____

4. Both students had a huge science project due the Monday of next week. Which student put it off until the end? _____

5. Which student is more likely to use time effectively? _____ Why? _____

   _____

6. How many hours did Janet spend on homework this week? _____

7. How many hours did Carlos spend on homework this week? _____

8. How many hours of homework a day did Carlos average over seven days? _____

Extensions

- On Monday, Justin rode his scooter for 2 ½ hours. He spent the following amounts of time on his scooter for the next six days: 3 hours, 1 ½ hours, ½ hour, 2 hours, 5 ½ hours, and 4 hours. Make a single line graph to illustrate how much time Justin rode each day of the week.

- Make a table estimating how many hours you slept in the last seven days. Then create a single-line graph from this table.

Facts to Know

Graphs are effective tools used to compare data in clear, concise, visual terms.

Three of the most common graphs are bar graphs, circle graphs (pie charts), and line graphs.

Pictograph

A *pictograph* uses pictures or symbols to compare data. It is useful for units where smaller numbers or even blocks of data are used. A key indicates the value of each symbol. Sometimes a symbol is cut in half to indicate half of the amount.

Survey by Category of Books Read by 200 8th Grade Students

fantasy	☐ ☐ ▯
science fiction	☐
humor	☐ ☐ ☐ ☐ ☐ ☐ ☐ ☐
romance	☐ ☐ ☐ ☐ ▯
true life	☐ ▯
mystery	☐ ☐ ▯

Key ☐ = 10 books

Multiple-line Graph

A *multiple-line graph* compares two or more sets of data, which are changing over time. Two lines are usually used to compare how two events might be related to each other and affect each other over a period of time.

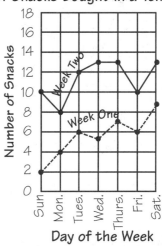

Number of Snacks Bought in a Ten-day Period

Double-Bar Graph

A *double bar graph* is used to compare two sets of data within a given period of time or set of circumstances.

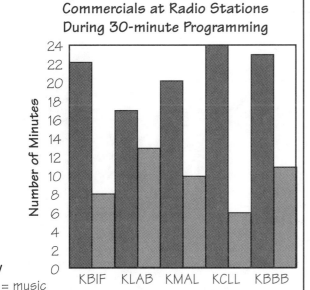

Minutes Devoted to Music and Commercials at Radio Stations During 30-minute Programming

Key
▓ = music
▒ = commercials

Histogram

A *histogram* is a diagram, which often illustrates the frequency of an event and shows how data falls into different intervals. The intervals, represented by rectangular bars, may be the same width or they may vary. Histograms are usually used with continuous data, which falls into varying intervals.

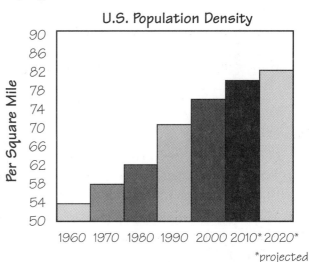

U.S. Population Density

*projected

•••••••••••• Working with Pictographs and Histograms

A pictograph uses pictures or symbols to illustrate data comparisons. This pictograph illustrates the life span of various types of garbage.

Life Span of Garbage

cardboard boxes	🗑 🗑 🗑 🗑	
camera film	🗑 🗑 🗑 🗑 🗑 🗑	
trash bags	🗑 🗑 🗑 🗑	
pantyhose	🗑 🗑 🗑 🗑 🗑 🗑 🗑 🗑	
soft-drink cans	🗑 🗑 🗑 🗑 🗑 🗑 🗑 🗑 🗑 🗑 🗑 🗑 🗑 🗑 🗑 🗑	
plastic bottles	🗑 🗑 🗑 🗑 🗑 🗑 🗑 🗑 🗑 🗑 🗑 🗑 🗑 🗑 🗑 🗑	
coated cartons	🗑 🗓	
leather shoes	🗑 🗑 🗑 🗑 🗑 🗑 🗑 🗑 🗑 🗑	

Key

🗑 = 5 years

🗓 = 2½ years

Directions: Use the information on page 13 and this pictograph to answer these questions.

1. How many years does it take a cardboard box to decay? _____

2. How many years does it take pantyhose to decay? _____

3. How many more years does it take plastic bottles to decay than it takes leather shoes? _____

4. Which two items take the longest to decay? _____
   How many years does each type take? _____

5. How long do plastic-coated cartons take to decay? _____

6. How would this pictograph help communicate the problems of landfills and the value of recycling in this country? _____

Directions: This histogram illustrates the frequency of graduation rates in a recent year and the states where this frequency occurs.

7. How many states have between 81% and 90% of its students graduating? _____

8. How many states have between 51% and 60% of its students graduating? _____

9. What percentage of students is graduating in 22 states? _____

10. How many states are represented in all?

    _____

11. About 65% of California's public high school students graduate. In what frequency is California recorded on the graph? _____

12. Vermont is the state with the highest graduation rate (89.9%). In what frequency is Vermont included on the graph? _____

13. How might this histogram be used by public officials? _____

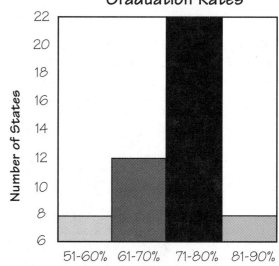

A **double-bar graph** is used to compare two sets of data. The double bar graph shown here illustrates the percentage of male/female attendance at several major colleges in the United States.

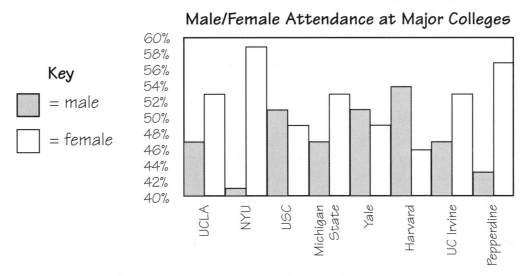

Male/Female Attendance at Major Colleges

Key
■ = male
□ = female

Directions: Use the information on page 13 and this graph to answer these questions.

1. What percentage of students at UCLA is male? _____ What percentage is female? _____

2. What percentage of students at Yale is male? _____ What percentage of students is female? _____

3. What percentage of students at NYU (New York University) is male? _____
   What percentage is female? _____

4. In which two colleges is the percentage of male and female students almost the same? _____

5. Which college has the greatest disparity between the percentage of male and female students?

   _____

6. What is the total percentage of male and female attendance at each college? _____
   Why? _____

7. Using the graph as a representative of college attendance, are more males or more females
   attending these colleges? _____

Directions: Study this double bar graph illustrating the points scored by two teams, the Bulldogs and the Wildcats, in the four quarters of a football game.

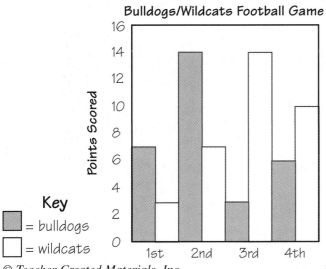

Bulldogs/Wildcats Football Game

Points Scored

Key
■ = bulldogs
□ = wildcats

8. What was the Bulldogs' best quarter? _____

9. What was the Wildcats' best quarter? _____

10. How many total points did each team score in
    the game? _____

11. Which team got better in the first three quarters?

    _____

12. How might a coach use this graph?

    _____

    _____

A **multiple-line graph** compares two or more sets of data, which are changing over time. This multiple-line graph illustrates the number of novel pages read each day for one week by two language arts students, Alyssa and Greg.

Directions: Use the information on page 13 and this graph to answer the following questions.

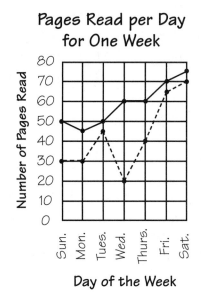

Pages Read per Day for One Week

Number of Pages Read

Day of the Week

Key

—— = Alyssa

------ = Greg

1. How many pages did Greg read on Sunday? _____

2. How many pages did Alyssa read on Sunday? _____

3. How many pages did Greg read on Friday? _____

4. How many pages did Alyssa read on Friday? _____

5. On which day did Greg read the fewest pages? _____

6. On which day did Alyssa read the fewest pages? _____

7. Which student read the most pages during the week?

    _____

8. How many more pages did Alyssa read than Greg on Monday? _____

9. On which three days did Alyssa read exactly five pages more than Greg? _____

10. How many total pages did Alyssa read? _____

11. How many total pages did Greg read? _____

12. Which student was more consistent in doing the assigned reading?_____

Directions: Study this graph illustrating how many minutes Sarah and Catherine practiced playing the piano in a period of six weeks. Answer the questions below.

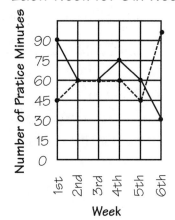

Minutes of Piano Practice Each Week for Six Weeks

Number of Pratice Minutes

Week

Key

—— = Sarah

------ = Catherine

13. How many minutes did Sarah practice the first week?

    _____

14. How many minutes did Catherine practice the first week? _____

15. How many minutes did Sarah practice for the entire six weeks? _____

16. How many minutes did Catherine practice for the entire six weeks? _____

17. Which student practiced more in the sixth week?

    _____

18. Did Catherine become a better or worse piano student during the six weeks?_____ Explain.

    _____

    _____

Facts to Know

Measures of Central Tendency

The *measures of central tendency* are different kinds of averages, which often effectively represent all of the numbers or values in a collection of data. These are numbers located close to the middle of a data collection. There are three measures of central tendency: the *mode*, the *median*, and the *mean*.

Mode

The *mode* is the most frequently occurring number in a set of numbers.

(65, 75, 80, (85,) (85,) (85,) (85,) (85,) 90, 95)

The most frequently occurring number is 85. The mode is 85.

- If one number occurs very often in a set of data, that number, the mode, often is the most representative number of that set and the most useful in analyzing the data.
- If two numbers occur with equal frequency, there is a bimodal pattern.

  (4, 6, 7, (8,) (8,) (8,) [9,] [9,] [9,] 10, 11, 14, 18)

The *modes* are 8 and 9.

Median

The *median* is the middle number in a set of data arranged from least to greatest.

- To determine the median with an odd number of values in a set of data, arrange the numbers in order from least to greatest. The middle number is the median.

  (1, 2, 3, 4, 5, 5, (6,) 7, 8, 9, 10, 12, 15)

  The middle number (median) is the 7th of 13 numbers.

  The *median* is 6.

- To determine the median with an even number of values in a set of data, arrange the numbers in order from least to greatest. Add the two middle numbers and divide the answer by 2.

  (56, 57, 60, 62, (63,) (66,) 68, 72, 73, 80)

  The 5th and 6th numbers are the two middle numbers—63 and 66

  63 + 66 = 129 and 129 divided by 2 is 64.5

  The median is 64.5 (even though it is not a number listed in the set).

- The median can be a very good average to use if the values in the middle of the data are fairly similar to each other.

Mean (Arithmetic Mean or Average)

The *mean* is the sum of the values in a set of data divided by the number of values in the set.

- To calculate the arithmetic mean, compute the sum of the values in a set of data and then divide the sum by the number of values.

  (3, 4, 6, 7, 8, 10, 11, 12, 13, 16)

  The sum of the numbers is 90.

  90 divided by 10 is 9.

  The *mean* is 9.

- When all of the numbers are relatively close in value, the mean is usually in the middle of the values and is an effective average to use.

4 ▶ Practice • • • • • • • Working with Mode and Median

The **mode** is the most frequently occurring number in a set of data.

- If the mode occurs in the middle of a set of numbers, it is often a useful way to describe the set of data.
- If the mode appears at the beginning or end of a set of data, it may be atypical and not very descriptive of this set of values.
- *Outliers* are numbers well above or below the other values in a set of data.

The **median** is the middle number in a set of data arranged from least to greatest.

- The median may be useful in describing a set of data with outliers at each end and numbers evenly distributed within the set of data.

Directions: Use the information on page 17 to help you find the mode and median in each set of data. Indicate why you think each mode and median is representative or not representative of the data.

1. A 7th grader's points scored for nine basketball games: 22, 19, 14, 28, 16, 9, 12, 23, 16

   Arranged in order: _____

   Mode: _____

   Is the mode representative? _____ Why? _____

   Median: _____

   Is the median representative? _____ Why? _____

2. Mouse weights (in grams): 10, 11, 9, 7, 31, 20, 38, 15, 18, 14, 21, 10, 14

   Arranged in order: _____

   Mode: _____

   Is the mode representative? _____ Why? _____

   Median: _____

   Is the median representative? _____ Why? _____

3. Butterfly wing spans (in millimeters): 70, 57, 28, 64, 48, 32, 25, 19, 28, 48, 44, 51

   Arranged in order: _____

   Mode: _____

   Is the mode representative? _____ Why? _____

   Median: _____

   Is the median representative? _____ Why? _____

4. Home run leader totals: 61, 70, 47, 48, 49, 49, 40, 49, 40, 47, 39, 37, 47, 31

   Arranged in order: _____

   Mode: _____

   Is the mode representative? _____ Why? _____

   Median: _____

   Is the median representative? _____ Why? _____

5. Words on a page: 220, 224, 232, 218, 115, 235, 115, 221, 214, 74, 227

   Arranged in order: _____

   Mode: _____

   Is the mode representative? _____ Why? _____

   Median: _____

   Is the median representative? _____ Why? _____

4 ▶ Practice •••••••• Working with Arithmetic Mean

The **mean** is the sum of the values in a set of data divided by the number of values in the set.

- To calculate the arithmetic mean, compute the sum of the values in a set of data and then divide the sum by the number of values.

> Major League RBI (Runs batted in) leader totals:
>
> (158, 140, 150, 128, 116, 123, 109, 117, 122)
>
> The sum is 1,163. 1,163 divided by 9 is 129.2   The *mean* is 129 (rounded off).

- When all of the numbers are relatively close in value, the mean is usually in the middle of the values and it is then an effective average to use.

- If one value is unusually high or low, it may affect the mean and make it less representative.

Directions: Use the information above and on page 17 to help you find the mean in each set of data. Remember to round off the mean. Indicate why you think each mean is representative or not representative of the data. The first one has been started for you.

1. Number of species in United States zoos:

   (699, 718, 650, 900, 590, 630, 607, 650, 750, 794)

   Total: <u>6,988</u>   Divide by: <u>10</u>   The mean is <u>698.8 (699).</u>

   Is the mean representative? <u>Yes</u> Why? _____

2. Number of moons for nine planets:

   (0, 0, 1, 2, 16, 22, 15, 8, 1)

   Total: _____   Divide by: _____   The mean is _____.

   Is the mean representative? _____ Why? _____

3. Wind speeds recorded in a two-week period:

   (25, 18, 22, 31, 12, 13, 12, 17, 19, 24, 19, 27, 28, 10)

   Total: _____   Divide by: _____   The mean is _____.

   Is the mean representative? _____ Why? _____

4. Temperatures recorded twice daily:

   (70, 95, 68, 78, 75, 92, 78, 84, 68, 85, 72, 83, 75, 90)

   Total: _____   Divide by: _____   The mean is _____.

   Is the mean representative? _____ Why? _____

5. Calories burned per hour in activities:

   (210, 80, 160, 220, 250, 140, 220, 180, 450, 225, 250, 210)

   Total: _____   Divide by: _____   The mean is _____.

   Is the mean representative? _____ Why? _____

6. Numbers rolled using two dice:

   (7, 6, 2, 7, 8, 3, 12, 9, 7, 4, 6, 7, 11, 6, 7, 10)

   Total: _____   Divide by: _____   The mean is _____.

   Is the mean representative? _____ Why? _____

It is important to recognize the **measures of central tendency** (*mode*, *median*, or *mean*), which is most representative of a set of data. Sometimes one of the measures is clearly the most useful. Sometimes two or three measures may be equally valuable.

- If all three numbers are identical or very close, you know the data is likely to be statistically valid.

> Daily high temperatures for a week: (79°, 80°, 81°, 78°, 79°, 82°, 77°)
> Mode: 79° Median: 79° Mean: 79.4° (79°, rounded off)

- A reading of 79° is clearly representative of this week's high temperatures.

Directions: Use the information on page 17 to help you find the mode, median, and mean in each set of data. Indicate which measure or measures you think is most representative of the data.

1. Number of dots on selected ladybugs:

   (15, 0, 7, 9, 13, 2, 13, 15, 16, 13, 9, 13, 0)

   Mode: _____ Median: _____ Mean: _____

   Most representative measure: _____

   Reason: _____

2. Number of candy-coated chocolates in small bags:

   (22, 24, 25, 22, 21, 26, 23, 22, 23, 23, 25, 24)

   Mode: _____ Median: _____ Mean: _____

   Most representative measure: _____

   Reason: _____

3. Length of red worms (in centimeters):

   (10, 8, 6, 5, 12, 8, 7, 9, 11, 8, 6, 9, 10, 8, 8)

   Mode: _____ Median: _____ Mean: _____

   Most representative measure: _____

   Reason: _____

4. Number of drops of water that will fit on a penny:

   (21, 40, 46, 34, 56, 46, 99, 65, 48, 38, 69, 54, 50, 61)

   Mode: _____ Median: _____ Mean: _____

   Most representative measure: _____

   Reason: _____

5. Number of drops of water that will fit on a dime:

   (40, 38, 42, 16, 23, 28, 44, 25, 41, 23, 45, 30, 29, 27)

   Mode: _____ Median: _____ Mean: _____

   Most representative measure: _____

   Reason: _____

5 ▶ How to • • • • • • • • • • Analyze and Interpret Data

Facts to Know

Here are some special tools for analyzing and interpreting the meaning of data, which has been organized into tables or plotted on a graph.

Trends

- A *trend* indicates the direction of the data. A *trend line* is often drawn within a set of points on a scattergram or graph to determine the direction of the data. A trend line is sometimes called a *line of best fit*. It will plot the general direction of a set of data.

- The trend lines in the graphs below indicate that sales of scooters increased and sales of skateboards declined in this store during an eight-month period.

Sales of Scooters and Skateboards at the A-to-Z Sports Emporium

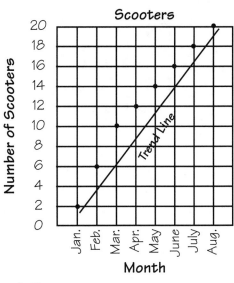

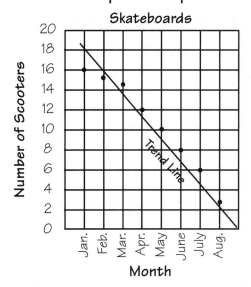

Correlation

- *Correlation* is an assessment of two pieces of data to determine how closely they are related or if they are related. A correlation between two sets of data may be weak or strong, depending on the data.

- *Positive correlation* indicates that an increase in one set of data leads to an increase in a second set of data.

- *Negative correlation* indicates that an increase in one set of data leads to decrease in another set of data.

    The graphs above indicate a strong negative correlation between the sales of scooters and skateboards in this store.

Extrapolation

- Use *extrapolation* to estimate or predict additional unknown data based on the trend of data you already know. Use the trend line on a graph to predict which data would probably come next. On the scooter graph, you can extrapolate that September's sales will probably continue to rise.

Interpolation

- Use *interpolation* to estimate a probable value for an unknown piece of data falling between two pieces of data. Use the trend line to make this estimate.

5 ▶ Practice •••••• Using Correlation, Extrapolation, and Interpolation

- A **scattergram** is made by plotting two sets of data as coordinate pairs on a graph.
- A **scattergram** is used so assess correlation. The closer the dots on the scattergram come to a straight line, the greater the correlation between the sets of data.

Directions: Study the scattergrams below. Use the information on page 21 to help you do this page.

1. How long did the students with the best language arts grades (90 or above) read? _____

2. How long did the students with the lowest grades (30 or below) read? _____

3. Is there a correlation between hours read and grades in this class? _____

4. Is the correlation weak or strong? _____

5. Is the correlation positive or negative? _____

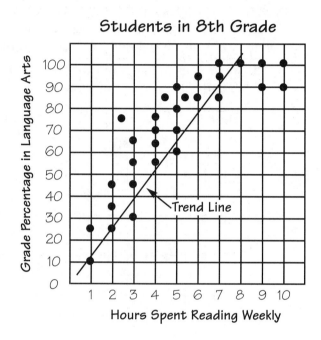

6. Draw a trend line to indicate the general direction of the trend indicated on the graph.

7. Is there a correlation between the number of five-gallon tubs of ice cream consumed and the temperature? _____

8. Is the correlation strong or weak? _____

9. Is the correlation positive or negative?

_____

10. Using interpolation, make an estimate for the number of tubs consumed on the day the temperature was 84°. _____

11. Using extrapolation, make an estimate for sales on the following days if the temperature pattern remains the same. _____

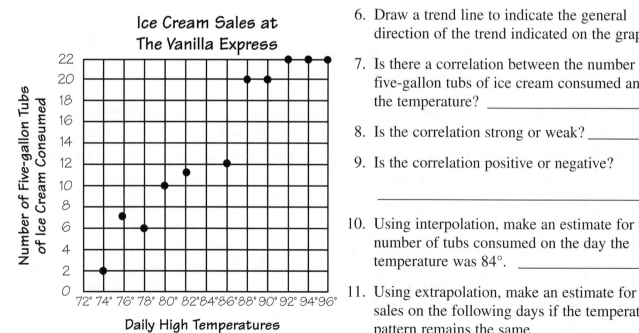

Directions: Use the scattergrams below and the information on page 21 to complete the page.

A basketball player graphed his shooting success from different distances from the basket. He took eight shots at each five-foot interval from the basket.

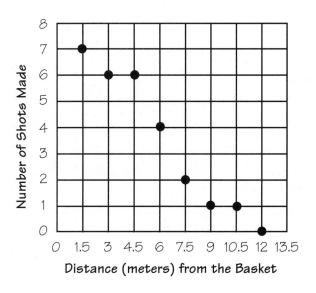

Distance (meters) from the Basket

1. How many shots did the player make five feet from the basket? _____

2. How many shots did the player make 25 feet from the basket? _____

3. Is there a correlation between shots made and distance? _____

4. Is the correlation weak or strong? _____

5. Is the correlation positive or negative? _____

6. Draw a trend line on the graph.

7. Extrapolating from the data given, how many of the eight shots would the player be likely to make two feet from the basket? _____

This scattergram relates the Science and Language Arts grades of 35 students.

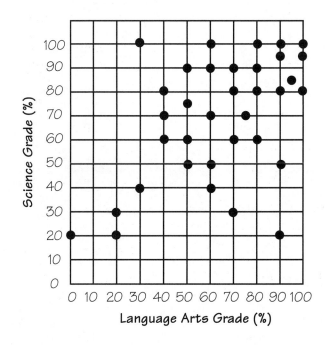

Language Arts Grade (%)

8. Draw a trend line through the scattergram.

9. Is there a strong correlation, a weak correlation, or no correlation between science and language arts grades in this group of students? _____

10. Are most students either strong in both subjects or weak in both subjects? _____

11. Would a student with good grades in science be likely or unlikely to do well in language arts? _____

Directions: Use the scattergrams and the information from page 21 to complete the page.

An 8th grader made a graph illustrating how many feet she ran in 15-second increments.

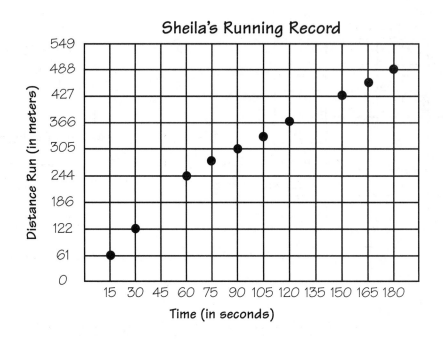

Sheila's Running Record

1. Draw a trend line on the graph indicating the direction of the data.

2. How many meters did Sheila run in 30 seconds? _____

3. How many meters did Sheila run in 60 seconds? _____

4. Using interpolation, determine about how many meters Sheila had run in 45 seconds. _____

5. Is the correlation between the number of meters run and the time strong or weak? _____

6. Is the correlation between the distance run and the time spent running positive or negative? _____

7. Extrapolating from the data given, about how far will Sheila have run in 195 seconds? _____

8. Extrapolating from the data given, about how far will Sheila have run in 210 seconds? _____

How to • • • • • • • • • Collect, Organize, Represent, and Interpret Your Data

Facts to Know

Data is all around you—in the classroom, on the playing field, at home, in every store, and many other places as well.

Collecting Data

- Use tally sheets, record sheets, or lists of data to record your information.
- Use almanacs, field guides, encyclopedias, or textbooks to find data on history or science.
- Use magazines, newspapers, or television news programs to find up-to-the-minute data about daily life.

Data Ideas

- passing percentages
- hitting/baseball
- grades/scores
- store sales
- calories taken in/expended
- basketball shooting scored
- heights or weights
- student food preferences
- time expended on . . .
- comparative prices

Organizing Data

- Use tables and charts to group your data according to size, time periods, amounts, or some other numerical pattern.

Representing Data

- Choose the best type of graph to represent your data in a clear, visual, and effective way.

Bar Graph	compares data in numerical chunks
Circle Graph	shows percentages of 100; parts of a whole
Line Graph	compares change over a period of time
Pictograph	symbols used to compare data
Histogram	compares data in varying intervals
Double Bar Graph	compares sets of related data
Multiple-line Graph	compares how two or more related sets of data change over a period of time
Scattergram	shows how pieces of data are related

Interpreting Data

- Use the measures of central tendency to determine various averages for sets of data.

    Mode—most frequently occurring number
    Median—the middle number in a set of data arranged from least to greatest
    Mean—the sum of the values divided by the number of values

- Look for the *trend line* or *line of best fit.*
- Use *interpolation* to find an unknown value within or between known pieces of data.
- Use *extrapolation* to find data beyond the values listed in a set of data.
- Look for *positive or negative correlation* to determine if two sets of data are actually related to each other.

Recognizing Misleading Statistics

- Study graphs to determine if they are truncated or designed to distort data.
- Use common sense to determine if sets of data are related or accidentally have the same pattern.

Directions: This bar graph illustrates the results of one 6th grade class survey of favorite exercises. Use the information on page 25 and the graph to answer these questions.

Favorite Exercises

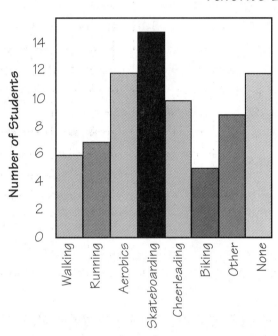

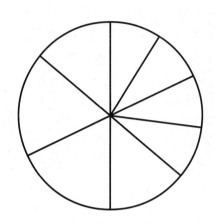

1. Which exercise was the most favorite? _____

2. Which two exercises together were as popular as skateboarding? _____

3. How many students were surveyed altogether? _____

4. What percentage of the total did not do any exercise? _____

5. Fill in the circle graph above with the same information. The lines are already drawn for you.

Directions: Write down an estimate of the number of hours you spent watching television in the last seven days. Round each number off to the nearest half-hour. Use the line graph below to illustrate your findings. Then do the following activities.

1. Describe how your television habits changed over time, the course of one week. Explain why some days had more or less hours than others.

   _____

   _____

2. Make this a multiple-line graph by recording your television watching for another seven days. Compare your results. Are the patterns similar or is there a large difference? _____

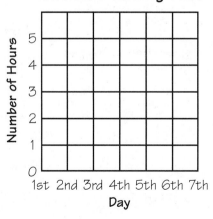

Television Viewing Time

Both the bar graph and the scattergram are misleading and can lead to misunderstanding the data.

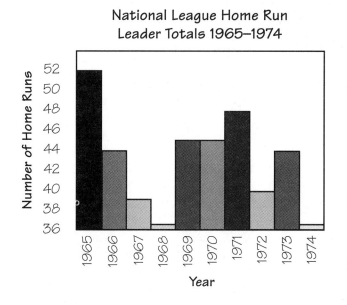

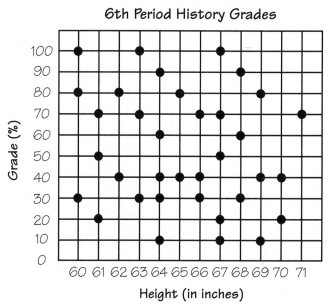

Directions: Use the information on page 25 and your careful examination of the graphs to answer these questions.

1. The graph makes it look as if the 1965 leader hit twice as many home runs as the 1966 leader. What is the actual difference? _____

2. The information on the home run scale is truncated. It begins with 36 home runs. How should the graph have been arranged? _____

3. Why do you think the scale was truncated? _____

4. Is there likely to be any relationship between height and history grades? _____

5. Is there any trend line on the scattergram? _____

Extension

- Survey the height (in inches) of 20 or more students.

- Survey each student's arm span from fingertip to fingertip (to the nearest inch).

- Record each student's information on a record sheet.

- Create a scattergram and graph the data on it (a dot for each individual). Use the vertical axis for the height and the horizontal axis for the arm span.

- Draw a trend line on your scattergram.

- Interpret your data by answering the following questions:

  What is the correlation between arm span and height?

  Why is there a correlation between arm span and height?

6 ▶ Practice •••••••••••• Applying the Measures of Central Tendency to Your Data

- A **line plot** has a scale along the horizontal reference line and each piece of data plotted above the appropriate number on the scale.
- A **line plot** will demonstrate the range of the data, the mode, and any outliners.

Line Plot of Hours Spent Sleeping for 36 Eighth Graders

```
                                          X           X
                                          X   X   X
                                          X   X   X
                                          X   X   X   X
                        X   X   X   X   X   X
                    X   X   X   X   X   X   X
    X   X       X   X   X   X   X   X   X   X           X
   ─────────────────────────────────────────────────────
    0   1   2   3   4   5   6   7   8   9  10  11  12
```

Directions: Use the information on page 25 and the line plot to answer these questions.

1. Complete this list of per student hours slept using the line plot above:

   (0, 1, 3, 4, 4, 5, 5, 5, ____, ____, ____, ____, ____, ____, ____, ____, ____, ____, ____, ____,

   ____, ____, ____, ____, ____, ____, ____, ____, ____, ____, ____, ____, ____, ____, ____,

   ____, ____, ____, ____, ____, ____, ____, ____, ____, ____, ____, ____, ____, ____, ____,)

2. How many students slept for nine hours? _____

3. How many students didn't sleep at all? _____

4. How many students slept three hours? _____

5. What are the three outliers in this set of data? (The pieces of data on the ends of the range of data.)_____

6. Which two hours are the modes of this data? _____

7. What is the median for all 36 students? _____

8. What is the mean for this data?_____

9. Are the mode, median, and mean close to each other?_____

10. Do you think these are valid statistics? _____ Explain. _____

Extension

Survey each member of your class to determine how many hours they sleep on an average night to the nearest hour.

- Use a tally sheet to record your answers.
- Make a numerical list of the answers from least to greatest.
- Create a line plot like the one above to graph your results.
- List any outliers.
- Determine the mode.

- Determine the median.
- Compute the mean.
- How close are the mode, median, and mean to each other?
- Do you think the statistics are valid and useful? Why or why not?

Facts to Know

Permutations

- A permutation is an arrangement of items in a particular order.
- If you change the order of the items, you produce another permutation.

  Sample A

  Arrange the letters X, Y, and Z as many different ways as you can.

X, Y, Z	Z, X, Y	Y, Z, X
Y, X, Z	X, Z, Y	Z, Y, X

  There are six different permutations using those three letters.

  The items are the same, but the order is different.

Tree Diagrams

A tree diagram can be used to illustrate all the possible permutations.

  Sample B

  How many different ways can you arrange a nickel (N), a dime (D), and a penny (P)?

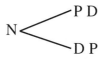 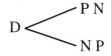 

Factorials

- A factorial can be used to determine the number of permutations involved with the order of objects.
- A factorial is identified by an exclamation mark (!). 3! is read as "three factorial."

  3! means 3 x 2 x 1 which equals 6.

  Sample C

  How many ways can you arrange 4 coins: quarter, dime, nickel, and penny?

  Four coins can be written as 4! (four factorial)

  4! = 4 x 3 x 2 x 1 = 24

  Four coins can be arranged in order in 24 different ways.

Combinations

- A combination is an arrangement of items where the order does not matter.

  In a combination, for example, XYZ is the same as ZYX or YZX.

- The counting principle is used to determine the number of possible combinations.

  If one event can happen in *A* ways and a second event can happen in *B* ways, both events can happen in *A* times *B* ways.

  Sample D

  You have three shirts (one red, one green, one blue) and two pairs of shorts (one blue and one green). How many different outfit combinations can you wear?

  3 (shirts) x 2 (pairs of shorts) = 6 (different outfits)

How many ways can you arrange one pen and one pencil?

You can have: pencil/pen or pen/pencil

Directions: Use the information on page 29 to help you do these problems.

1. Make a tree diagram to illustrate the different ways
   you can arrange a math book, a reading text, and a
   dictionary. What is the total number of ways?

2. Complete this chart to illustrate all of the possible ways to arrange these letters: A, B, C, and D.

A B C D	B A C D	C ___ ___ ___	D ___ ___ ___
A B D C	B A ___ ___	___ ___ ___ ___	___ ___ ___ ___
A C B D	B ___ ___ ___	___ ___ ___ ___	___ ___ ___ ___
A C D B	___ ___ ___ ___	___ ___ ___ ___	___ ___ ___ ___
A D C B	___ ___ ___ ___	___ ___ ___ ___	___ ___ ___ ___
A D B C	___ ___ ___ ___	___ ___ ___ ___	___ ___ ___ ___

3. Use a factorial to show how many ways the four letters can be arranged.

   4! = 4 x 3 x ___ x ___

   How many ways can you arrange the letters? _____

4. You have five trophies for these sports: baseball, basketball, soccer, football, and swimming. Use a factorial to determine how many different ways you can arrange them in order.

   5! = 5 x ___ x ___ x ___ x ___

   How many ways can you arrange the trophies? _____

5. You have six pieces of paper money: $1 bill, $2 bill, $5 bill, $10 bill, $20 bill, and $50 bill. Use a factorial to illustrate how many different arrangements you can use with these bills in your wallet.

   6! = ___ x ___ x ___ x ___ x ___ x ___

   How many ways can you arrange these six bills? _____

6. A girl has seven charms for her charm bracelet: a teddy bear, a heart, a ring, a cupid, a pearl, a doll, and a rose. Use a factorial to illustrate how many different ways she can order these charms on her bracelet.

   7! = _____

   How many different ways can she arrange them? _____

7. Martha has ten different dolls. She keeps them in a straight line on a shelf in her room. She places them in a different order every night. How many different arrangements can she make without repeating one? Use a factorial to find the answer.

   10! = _____

   How many different ways can she arrange her dolls? _____

Jennifer has three blouses (one blue, one yellow, and one white). She has three slacks (one black, one brown, and one blue). What is the total number of outfit combinations she can make without repeating one?

3 (blouses) x 3 (pairs of pants) = 9 (different outfits)

She can make nine different outfits.

Directions: Use the information on page 29 to help you do the problems.

1. You have three pens (one ballpoint, one gel, and one fountain pen). You have four pencils (one red, one black, one blue, and one green). How many combinations of two (one pencil and one pen) can you make? _____

2. You have a choice of five flavors of ice cream (vanilla, chocolate, strawberry, raspberry, and chocolate chip) and two serving methods (cone or dish). How many combinations of one ice cream flavor and one serving method can you have? _____

3. Your wardrobe includes five different shirts, four different pants, and two different pairs of shoes. How many different outfits consisting of shirt, pants, and shoes can you make? _____

4. You have a choice of eight different candy bars and seven different ice cream flavors at a party. How many combinations of one ice cream flavor and one candy bar can you have? _____

Directions: Study the example shown here and then do the problems below.

There are four flavors of ice cream at a party (vanilla, chocolate, strawberry, and peppermint). You have a choice of having any two different flavors. How many different combinations of ice cream flavors can you have? Answer: six combinations.

Possible choices: vanilla + chocolate; vanilla + strawberry; vanilla + peppermint; chocolate + strawberry; chocolate + peppermint; strawberry + peppermint

5. A fifth flavor, peach, was added to the four flavors in the problem above. You have a choice of having any two different flavors. How many different combinations of ice cream flavors can you have? _____

   Possible choices: _____

   _____

6. How many different combinations of ice cream flavors can you have if you can have any three of the five flavors in problem #5? _____

   Possible choices: _____

   _____

7. There are six different party favor choices: a whistle, a horn, a toy ring, a giant balloon, a squirt gun, and a mini-car. You can have any two favors. How many different combinations of party favors can you have? _____

   Possible choices: _____

   _____

Permutations and **combinations** are very useful in studying probability. They can be used to figure out all the possible things that can happen in a given situation.

> What is the probability of two heads landing when you flip two coins, a penny and a nickel, at one time?
>
> Possible outcomes:
> penny (head); nickel (head)
> penny (tail); nickel (tail)
> penny (head); nickel (tail)
> penny (tail); nickel (head)
>
> Probability of two heads: 1 in 4 or 1/4

Directions: Use the information on page 29 to help you do these problems. List the possible outcomes for each problem. The first one is done for you.

1. What is the probability of a penny landing heads when you flip it?

   Possible outcomes: *head or tail*

   Probability of heads: *1 in 2 or 1/2*

2. What is the probability of rolling a 4 with one die?

   Possible outcomes: _____

   Probability of rolling a 4: _____

3. What is the probability of rolling a 6 with one die?

   Possible outcomes: _____

   Probability of rolling a 6: _____

4. What is the probability of rolling a 4 or a 6 with one die?

   Possible outcomes: _____

   Probability of rolling a 4 or 6: _____

5. A black cloth bag holds one red marble, one green marble, one blue marble, and one black marble. All are the same size. Without looking into the bag, what is the probability of drawing a black marble from the bag?

   Possible outcomes: _____

   Probability of drawing the black marble:

   _____

6. What is the probability of drawing either the black or the blue marble from the bag?

   Possible outcomes: _____

   Probability of drawing the black or blue marble: _____

7. What is the probability of drawing a white marble?

   Possible outcomes: _____

   Probability of drawing a white marble:

   _____

8. What is the probability of drawing either the black, the green, or the blue marble from the bag?

   Possible outcomes: _____

   Probability of drawing the black, green, or blue marble: _____

9. What is the probability of one head and one tail landing when you flip two coins, a penny and a nickel, at the same time?

   Possible outcomes: _____

   Probability of one head and one tail:

   _____

Facts to Know

Theoretical Probability

If you use a formula to determine the probability of an outcome, you are working with **theoretical probability**.

- *Theoretical probability* can only be computed if the outcomes are all equally likely to occur.
- *Theoretical probability* can be used with things such as dice rolls or coin flips where the outcomes are equally likely to occur.
- *Theoretical probability* cannot be used where outcomes do not have an equal likelihood of occurring. Throwing a bat into the air and noting which way it lands would not allow the use of theoretical probability because the position of the bat as it lands is unpredictable.
- A formula for theoretical probability can be written this way:

$$\frac{number\ of\ desired\ outcomes}{number\ of\ possible\ outcomes}$$

(The number of desired outcomes is divided by the number of possible outcomes.)

Sample A

If a penny is flipped in the air, what is the probability that it will land heads?

$$\frac{number\ of\ desired\ outcomes\ (heads))}{number\ of\ possible\ outcomes\ (heads\ or\ tails)} = \frac{1}{2}$$

The probability of flipping heads is 1 in 2. It can be expressed as 1/2 or 0.50 or 50%.

Expressing Probability

- Probability is usually expressed as a *fraction*, a *decimal*, or a *percent*.
- The range of probable outcomes is expressed between 0 and 1 on a number line.
- If there is no possible outcome, the probability is 0. There is 0 probability of flipping both heads and tails on one flip of a penny.
- If the event is certain to happen, the probability is 100%. There is a 100% probability (or a probability of 1) that a flipped penny will land either heads or tails.

Sample B

What is the probability of landing on the A space with this spinner?

There is 1 chance in 4. It can be expressed as 1/4 or 0.25 or 25%.

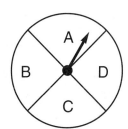

Experimental Probability

- You can determine the probability of an event by doing an experiment.
- The more often the experiment is done, the closer the results come to theoretical probability.
- This formula for experimental probability is expressed as:

$$\frac{number\ of\ times\ the\ desired\ outcome\ actually\ happened}{number\ of\ times\ the\ activity\ was\ done}$$

Flip a penny six times. Record the results.

1. _____   3._____   5. _____

2. _____   4._____   6. _____

How many times did it land heads? _____   How many times did it land tails?_____

The theoretical probability that the penny would land heads up was 1/2, so it should have landed heads three times.

Directions: Use the information on page 33 to help you do these problems.

Flip a penny 24 times. Record the results in the spaces provided.

1. _____   5. _____   9. _____   13. _____   17. _____   21. _____

2. _____   6. _____   10. _____   14. _____   18. _____   22. _____

3. _____   7. _____   11. _____   15. _____   19. _____   23. _____

4. _____   8. _____   12. _____   16. _____   20. _____   24. _____

How many times did the penny land heads? _____

The theoretical probability of a penny landing heads is 1/2 or 50%.

What was the experimental probability of the penny landing heads in this activity? ____ /24 or ____ %

Flip the penny 24 more times. Record the results.

25. _____   29. _____   33._____   37. _____   41. _____   45. _____

26. _____   30. _____   34._____   38. _____   42. _____   46. _____

27. _____   31. _____   35._____   39. _____   43. _____   47. _____

28. _____   32. _____   36._____   40. _____   44. _____   48. _____

How many times did the penny land heads in the 48 times it was flipped? _____

The theoretical probability of a penny landing heads is 1/2 or 50%.

What was the experimental probability of the penny landing heads after 48 trials? ____ /48 or ____ %

Flip the penny 24 more times. Record the results.

49. _____   53. _____   57._____   61. _____   65. _____   69. _____

50. _____   54. _____   58._____   62. _____   66. _____   70. _____

51. _____   55. _____   59._____   63. _____   67. _____   71. _____

52. _____   56. _____   60._____   64. _____   68. _____   72. _____

How many times did the penny land heads in the 72 times it was flipped? _____

What was the experimental probability of the penny landing heads after 72 trials? ____ /72 or ____ %

How close was this to the theoretical probability of 1/2 or 50%?_____

More with Experimental and Theoretical Probability

Roll the die six times. Record the results.

1. _____ 2. _____ 3. _____ 4. _____ 5. _____ 6. _____

How many times did you roll a 4? _____

The theoretical probability that you would roll a 4 is 1 in 6 or 1/6 or 16.6%.

The theoretical probability that you would roll any particular number from 1 to 6 is 1 in 6 or 1/6 or 16.6%.

Directions: Use the information on page 33 to help you do these problems.

Roll one die 24 times. Record the results.

1. _____ 5. _____ 9. _____ 13. _____ 17. _____ 21. _____
2. _____ 6. _____ 10. _____ 14. _____ 18. _____ 22. _____
3. _____ 7. _____ 11. _____ 15. _____ 19. _____ 23. _____
4. _____ 8. _____ 12. _____ 16. _____ 20. _____ 24. _____

Total your results and record the number of times you rolled:

1 ____ 2 ____ 3 ____ 4 ____ 5 ____ 6 ____

The theoretical probability that you would roll a specific number is 1 in 6 or 1/6 or 16.6%. This would be four times for each number. What was the actual experimental probability in this activity?

#1 ____ /24 or ____ %   #3 ____ /24 or ____ %   #5 ____ /24 or ____ %

#2 ____ /24 or ____ %   #4 ____ /24 or ____ %   #6 ____ /24 or ____ %

Did you roll any particular number a lot more or a lot less than four times? ____ Which number? ____

Roll one die 24 more times. Record the results.

25. _____ 29. _____ 33. _____ 37. _____ 41. _____ 45. _____
26. _____ 30. _____ 34. _____ 38. _____ 42. _____ 46. _____
27. _____ 31. _____ 35. _____ 39. _____ 43. _____ 47. _____
28. _____ 32. _____ 36. _____ 40. _____ 44. _____ 48. _____

Total your results for all 48 rolls and record the number of times you rolled:

1 ____ 2 ____ 3 ____ 4 ____ 5 ____ 6 ____

The theoretical probability that you would roll a specific number is 1 in 6 or 1/6 or 16.6%. This would be eight times for each number. What was the actual experimental probability in this activity?

#1 ____ /48 or ____ %   #3 ____ /48 or ____ %   #5 ____ /48 or ____ %

#2 ____ /48 or ____ %   #4 ____ /48 or ____ %   #6 ____ /48 or ____ %

Did you roll any particular number a lot more or a lot less than eight times? ____ Which one? ____

Roll one die 24 more times. Record the results.

49. _____ 53. _____ 57. _____ 61. _____ 65. _____ 69. _____
50. _____ 54. _____ 58. _____ 62. _____ 66. _____ 70. _____
51. _____ 55. _____ 59. _____ 63. _____ 67. _____ 71. _____
52. _____ 56. _____ 60. _____ 64. _____ 68. _____ 72. _____

What was the actual experimental probability in this activity?

#1 ____ /72 or ____ %   #3 ____ /72 or ____ %   #5 ____ /72 or ____ %

#2 ____ /72 or ____ %   #4 ____ /72 or ____ %   #6 ____ /72 or ____ %

Did you roll any particular number a lot more or a lot less than 12 times? ____ Which number? ____

•••••••• **Even More with Experimental and Theoretical Probability**

Directions: Use the information on page 33 to help you do these problems. Use a pair of dice of two different colors, if possible, or mark one **L** and the other **D**.

1. Use a pair of dice to help you complete this chart. Consider one die light and the other one dark.

Possible Rolls of Two Dice

L = light die   D = dark die

Possible Rolls					Total
2 → L1 D1					1
3 → L1 D2 – L2 D1					2
4 → L2 D2 – L1 D3 – L3 D1					3
5 → L1 D4 – L4 D1 – L2 D3 – L3 D2					4
6 → ____	____	____	____	____	____
7 → ____	____	____	____	____	____	____
8 → ____	____	____	____	____	____
9 → ____	____	____	____		____
10 → ____	____	____			____
11 → ____	____				____
12 → ____					____

2. What are the total possible rolls with two dice? _____

3. What is the theoretical probability of rolling a 2 expressed as a fraction? ___ as a percentage?___

4. What is the theoretical probability of rolling a 3 expressed as a fraction? ___ as a percentage?___

5. What is the theoretical probability of rolling a 5 expressed as a fraction? ___ as a percentage?___

6. What is the theoretical probability of rolling a 7 expressed as a fraction? ___ as a percentage?___

7. What is the theoretical probability of rolling a 9 expressed as a fraction? ___ as a percentage?___

8. What is the theoretical probability of rolling a 12 expressed as a fraction? ___ as a percentage?___

Directions: Roll two dice 36 times. Record the results below. Then complete the activities that follow.

1._____	7._____	13._____	19._____	25._____	31._____
2._____	8._____	14._____	20._____	26._____	32._____
3._____	9._____	15._____	21._____	27._____	33._____
4._____	10._____	16._____	22._____	28._____	34._____
5._____	11._____	17._____	23._____	29._____	35._____
6._____	12._____	18._____	24._____	30._____	36._____

Total the number of times you rolled:

2 ____ 3 ____ 4 ____ 5 ____ 6 ____ 7 ____ 8 ____ 9 ____ 10 ____ 11 ____ 12 ____

Create a bar graph to illustrate the results.

•• Work with Probability in Independent, Dependent, and Compound Events

Facts to Know

Probability with Independent Events

- Two outcomes are *independent* if what happens in one has no relationship to what happens in the other.
- Two or more independent events have no affect on each other.
- To determine the probability of two independent events occurring, multiply the probability of one event occurring times the probability of the second event occurring.

> The formula to express this is: Probability of A + B = Probability of A x B.

- Probabilities are usually multiplied in their decimal or fractional expressions.

Sample A

The probability that a student in Arrow Valley Middle School likes ice cream is 3/4 or 0.75 or 75%.

The probability that a student likes to play baseball is 1/5 or 0.20 or 20%.

The fact that a student likes to eat ice cream and play baseball is not related.

The probability that a student likes both ice cream and playing baseball is determined by multiplying 3/4 times 1/5 or 0.75 times 0.20.

The answer is 3/20 or 0.15 or 15%.

Probability with Dependent Events

- Two outcomes are *dependent* if what happens to one determines what happens to the other.
- The first outcome in two dependent events directly affects the outcome of the second event.
- To determine the probability of two dependent events occurring, multiply the probability of the first times the probability of the second, taking into account what has happened in the first outcome.

> The formula to express this is: Probability of A + B = Probability of A x B
> (given what happened in A).

Sample B

A box of ten crayons has two reds, two blues, two oranges, two greens, and two yellows.

What is the probability that you will choose a red both times? The probability of choosing a red the first time is 2/10. The second outcome is dependent on the first. The probability of choosing a red the second time is 1/9. (You only have one red crayon left and nine crayons altogether.)

Multiply 2/10 times 1/9. The answer is 2/90, which equals 1/45 or about 2%.

Probability with Compound Events

- *Compound* events or *combined* events involve putting together two or more events.
- The probability of two compound events is found by adding the probability of each event.

> The formula is expressed this way: Probability of A or B equals the Probability of A + the
> Probability of B.

- Compound events are usually indicated by the word "or."

Directions: Use the information on page 37 to help you solve these problems.

> ### Sample
>
> A survey of 60 seventh graders found that 3/4 of them liked pepperoni pizza. The same survey found that 2/3 of them liked to ride scooters.
>
> These events are independent of each other. To determine the probability that a student likes both pepperoni pizza and riding scooters, multiply 3/4 times 2/3. There is a 1/2 or 50% probability that a student likes both pepperoni pizza and riding scooters.

1. A survey of 75 eighth graders at Arrow Valley Middle School found that 2/5 of the students liked vanilla ice cream. The same survey discovered that 1/3 of the students liked art. What is the probability that a student liked both vanilla ice cream and art? _____

2. There were 100 sixth graders in Arrow Valley School. When asked, 17/20 of the sixth graders liked candy and 4/5 of the sixth graders liked to ride roller coasters. What is the probability that a student liked both candy and riding roller coasters? _____

3. A group of seventh graders were doing math projects where 4/7 of them flipped pennies and 5/6 of them rolled dice. What is the probability that a student both flipped pennies and rolled dice?

   _____

4. A soccer team went to an amusement park where 9/10 of them rode roller coasters and 1/2 of them went to shooting galleries. What is the probability both rode roller coasters and went to shooting galleries? _____

5. A large group of Girl Scouts went on a weekend camp out where 7/10 of them went hiking and 4/5 of them went swimming. What is the probability that a Girl Scout both went hiking and swimming? _____

6. A group of sixth graders went to science camp for a week where 9/10 of them went hiking, 4/5 went night hiking, and 2/3 of them studied the stars. What is the probability that a student participated in all three activities? _____

7. A group of science students went to a college for a week where 2/3 studied chemistry, 3/4 studied physics, and 9/10 studied earth science. What is the probability that a student studied all three subjects that week? _____

8. On a baseball team, 9/10 of the players got to hit, 1/4 of the players got to pitch, and 1/3 of the players got to play in the outfield. What is the probability that a player got to hit, pitch, and play in the outfield? _____

9. On a basketball team, 3/4 of the team scored at least one field goal, 2/3 of the team made a foul shot, and 1/2 of the team grabbed a rebound. What is the probability that a player scored a field goal, made a foul shot, and grabbed a rebound? _____

There are three marbles (one red, one green, and one blue) in a black bag. What is the probability of drawing a red marble out of the bag on the first attempt and, if the red is drawn out, drawing a green marble out of the bag on the second attempt?

★ These are dependent events. The second event is dependent upon the first.

★ The probability of drawing the red marble on the first attempt is 1/3.

★ If the red marble is drawn out and kept out, the probability of drawing the green marble on the second attempt is 1/2. (There are only two marbles left.)

★ The probability of both events occurring is expressed this way:

Probability of A and B = Probability of A times the Probability of B (given that A occurs). Therefore, 1/3 x 1/2 = 1/6.

There is a 1/6 probability of drawing the red on the first attempt and the green on the second attempt, given that the red marble was drawn on the first attempt.

Directions: Use the information on page 37 to help you do these problems.

1. There are four marbles (one red, one green, one blue, and one yellow) in a black bag. What is the probability of drawing a blue marble on the first try and, given that the blue marble is drawn and removed, drawing a green marble on the second try?

   A. Probability of blue on first try: _____

   B. Probability of green on the second try (given A): _____

   C. Probability of A and B (given A): _____ x _____ = _____ or _____%

2. A basket has the following names: Nancy, Nancy, James, Robert, and Juan. Two winners' names will be drawn from the basket. What is the probability of drawing Nancy's name both times?

   A. Probability of Nancy of the first draw: _____

   B. Probability of Nancy on the second draw (given A): _____

   C. Probability of A and B (given A): _____ x _____ = _____ or _____%

3. A black bag has 7 dollar bills, 2 five-dollar bills, and 1 ten-dollar bill. A contestant can draw two bills from the bag. What is the probability of drawing a five-dollar bill both times?

   A. Probability of a five on the first draw: _____

   B. Probability of a five on the second draw (given A): _____

   C. Probability of A and B (given A): _____ x _____ = _____ or _____%

4. A contestant can draw two times form a bag with 10 one-dollar bills, 5 five-dollar bills, 3 ten-dollar bills, and 2 twenty-dollar bills. What is the probability of drawing a twenty-dollar bill on both draws?

   A. Probability of a twenty-dollar bill on the first draw: _____

   B. Probability of a twenty-dollar bill on the second draw (given A): _____

   C. Probability of A and B (given A): _____ x _____ = _____ or _____%

5. A contestant chose two presents from eight identical boxes. There are two watches, five old rings, and one solid gold bracelet. What is the probability of getting the bracelet on the first choice and a watch on the second choice?

   A. Probability of the bracelet on first choice: _____

   B. Probability of a watch on the second choice (given A): _____

   C. Probability of A and B (given A): _____ x _____ = _____ or _____%

Directions: Use the information on page 37 to help you do these problems.

Sample

Everyone in a class of 20 science students has an opportunity to have his or her name drawn for a special field trip to a space museum. Bob and Sue are both in the class.

★ What is the probability that Bob's name will be drawn?
Answer: 1/20

★ What is the probability that Sue's name will be drawn?
Answer: 1/20

★ What is the probability that Bob or Sue's names will be drawn?
Answer: Probability of Bob or Sue = Probability of Bob + the Probability of Sue
Therefore, 1/20 + 1/20 = 2/20 or 1/10

---

1. A school fund-raiser sold exactly 600 raffle tickets. The winner will receive a new top of the line scooter. Jared bought 13 raffle tickets. Lewis bought 10 raffle tickets.

   What is the probability that Jared will win the scooter? _____

   What is the probability that Lewis will win the scooter? _____

   What is the probability that Jared or Lewis will win the scooter? _____

2. Julie bought 17 of the raffle tickets. Elaine bought only two of the tickets.

   What is the probability that Elaine will win the scooter? _____

   What is the probability that Julie will win the scooter? _____

   What is the probability that Julie or Elaine will win the scooter? _____

3. Using a die with the numbers 1 to 6 on it, what is the probability of rolling a 4? _____

   What is the probability of rolling a 4 or a 5? _____

   What is the probability of rolling a 1, a 5, or a 6? _____

   What is the probability of rolling a 2, a 3, a 4, or a 6? _____

4. Using a dodecahedral die with the numbers 1 to 12 on the 12 sides, what is the probability of rolling an 8? _____

   What is the probability of rolling a 4 or a 7? _____

   What is the probability of rolling a 3, an 8, or an 11? _____

   What is the probability of rolling a 1, a 2, a 3, a 4, or a 7? _____

5. Using a deck of 52 cards, what is the probability of drawing an Ace? _____

   What is the probability of drawing a Jack or a Queen? _____

   What is the probability of drawing a King, a Queen, or a Jack? _____

   What is the probability of drawing a face card or an Ace?_____

   What is the probability of drawing either a 9 or an 8? _____

   What is the probability of drawing a card worth less than 10? (In this situation, aces are worth more than 10.) _____

•••••••••••••••••• **Working with Data to Determine Probability**

You can use data to make predictions about the likelihood of an event occurring.

Directions: Use your understanding of probability and the pie chart to make predictions based on sales in the previous year. Express probabilities in fractions.

Sales at Chuck's Burgers

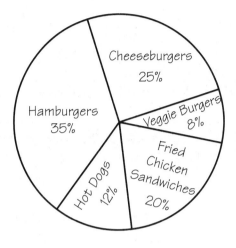

1. What is the probability that Chuck's next customer will buy a hamburger? _____

2. What is the probability that his next customer will buy a hot dog? _____

3. What is the likelihood that his next customer will buy either a hamburger or a cheeseburger? _____

4. What is the probability that the next customer will purchase either a fried chicken sandwich or a cheeseburger? _____

5. Of the next 100 customers at Chuck's, how many are likely to buy veggie burgers? _____

6. Of the next 1,000 customers, how many are likely to buy hamburgers? _____

7. If Chuck has 10,000 customers in the next six months, how many will get fried chicken sandwiches or hamburgers? _____

A survey of 30 seventh graders was conducted to determine the average amount of time each spent on the phone compared with their grade point averages. The results are plotted on this scattergram.

Directions: Study the graph and answer the questions.

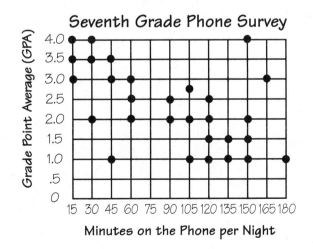

Seventh Grade Phone Survey

8. Draw a trend line on the scattergram indicating the direction of the data.

9. Is the correlation between the number of minutes on the phone and a GPA strong or weak? _____

10. Is the correlation between talking on the phone a long time and a high GPA positive or negative? _____

11. There were four students who didn't fit the pattern at all. What were their GPA/minutes on the phone coordinates?

    ____ / ____ min.   ____ / ____ min.

    ____ / ____ min.   ____ / ____ min.

12. Do most of the top students spend much time on the phone? _____

Look at the spinner below, next to the first set of questions. There are eight spaces. Each is the same size. Four spaces are dark. Four spaces are light.

What is the probability of landing on a dark space? The probability is 4/8 or 1/2 because half of the spaces on the spinner are dark.

Directions: Use the spinner on the left to answer these questions.

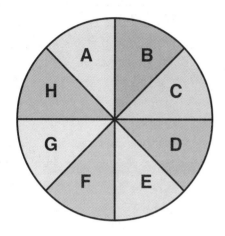

1. What is the probability of landing on space A? _____

2. What is the probability of landing on a light space? _____

3. What is the probability of landing on either space A or B? _____

4. What is the probability of landing on either space G or H? _____

5. What is the probability of landing on either a dark or light space? _____

6. What is the probability of landing on any space? _____

Directions: Use the dartboard on the right to answer these questions. Use fractions or percentages to express probability.

7. What is the probability of hitting space A on this dartboard? _____

8. What is the probability of hitting space C on this dartboard? _____

9. What is the probability of hitting space A or D on this dartboard? _____

10. What is the probability of hitting space B or C on this dartboard? _____

11. What is the probability of hitting space A, B, or C on this dartboard? _____

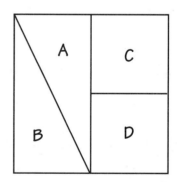

Directions: Use the dartboard on the left to answer these questions. Use fractions or percentages to express probability.

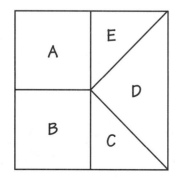

12. What is the probability of hitting space A on this dartboard? _____

13. What is the probability of hitting space D on this dartboard? _____

14. What is the probability of hitting space A or D on this dartboard? _____

15. What is the probability of hitting space C or E on this dartboard? _____

16. What is the probability of hitting space D, C, or E on this dartboard? _____

Directions: After recording 120 rolls of three dice, create a bar graph on another sheet of paper to illustrate the results.

Roll three dice 40 times. Record the results.

1. _____	8. _____	15. _____	22. _____	29. _____	35. _____
2. _____	9. _____	16. _____	23. _____	30. _____	36. _____
3. _____	10. _____	17. _____	24. _____	31. _____	37. _____
4. _____	11. _____	18. _____	25. _____	32. _____	38. _____
5. _____	12. _____	19. _____	26. _____	33. _____	39. _____
6. _____	13. _____	20. _____	27. _____	34. _____	40. _____
7. _____	14. _____	21. _____	28. _____		

Total your results for all 40 rolls and record them below.

3 _____	5 _____	7 _____	9 _____	11 _____	13 _____	15 _____	17 _____
4 _____	6 _____	8 _____	10 _____	12 _____	14 _____	16 _____	18 _____

Roll three dice 40 more times. Record the results.

41. _____	48. _____	55. _____	62. _____	69. _____	75. _____
42. _____	49. _____	56. _____	63. _____	70. _____	76. _____
43. _____	50. _____	57. _____	64. _____	71. _____	77. _____
44. _____	51. _____	58. _____	65. _____	72. _____	78. _____
45. _____	52. _____	59. _____	66. _____	73. _____	79. _____
46. _____	53. _____	60. _____	67. _____	74. _____	80. _____
47. _____	54. _____	61. _____	68. _____		

Total the results for this set of 40 rolls and record them below.

3 _____	5 _____	7 _____	9 _____	11 _____	13 _____	15 _____	17 _____
4 _____	6 _____	8 _____	10 _____	12 _____	14 _____	16 _____	18 _____

Roll three dice 40 more times. Record the results.

81. _____	88. _____	95. _____	102. _____	109. _____	116. _____
82. _____	89. _____	96. _____	103. _____	110. _____	117. _____
83. _____	90. _____	97. _____	104. _____	111. _____	118. _____
84. _____	91. _____	98. _____	105. _____	112. _____	119. _____
85. _____	92. _____	99. _____	106. _____	113. _____	120. _____
86. _____	93. _____	100. _____	107. _____	114. _____	
87. _____	94. _____	101. _____	108. _____	115. _____	

Total your results for this set of 40 rolls and record them below.

3 _____	5 _____	7 _____	9 _____	11 _____	13 _____	15 _____	17 _____
4 _____	6 _____	8 _____	10 _____	12 _____	14 _____	16 _____	18 _____

Total your results for the 120 rolls and record them here.

3 _____	5 _____	7 _____	9 _____	11 _____	13 _____	15 _____	17 _____
4 _____	6 _____	8 _____	10 _____	12 _____	14 _____	16 _____	18 _____

Odds is another term used to express probability from the point of view of desirable to undesirable outcomes.

★ A spinner can have three equal spaces (red, yellow, or green). If you wish to land on the red space, the odds in favor of that are expressed as 1 in 3, 1/3, or 1:3.

★ The odds against landing on the red space are 2 to 1 or 2/1 or 2:1 because there are two undesirable outcomes to one desirable outcome.

★ Use these formulas to help you compute the odds on this page.

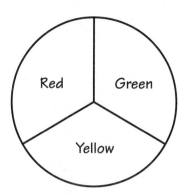

Odds in favor of an event = number of desirable outcomes / number of possible outcomes

Odds against an event = number of undesirable outcomes / number of desirable outcomes

Directions: Use the spinner on the right to compute the odds in these problems.

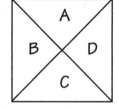

1. What are the odds of the spinner landing on section A? _____
2. What are the odds against the spinner landing on section A? _____
3. What are the odds of the spinner landing on sections A or C? _____
4. What are the odds against the spinner landing on sections A or C? _____
5. What are the odds of the spinner landing on sections A, B, or C? _____
6. What are the odds against the spinner landing on sections A, B, or C? _____

Directions: Compute these odds that have to do with the roll of a die.

7. What are the odds in favor of rolling a 6 with one die? _____
8. What are the odds against rolling a 6 with one die? _____
9. What are the odds in favor of rolling a 2 or 3 with one die? _____
10. What are the odds against rolling a 2 or 3 with one die? _____

Directions: Compute these odds concerning your chance of winning.

11. A sweepstakes has 500 entries. You have entered once. What are the odds in favor of you winning the sweepstakes? _____

12. What are the odds against you winning the sweepstakes? _____

13. A lottery sells 1,000,000 tickets. You have bought three tickets. What are your odds in favor of winning the lottery? _____

14. What are your odds against winning the lottery? _____

12 **Real Life** • • • • • • • • • • • • **Recognizing and Working with Misleading Statistics**

Some graphs are designed to create a false impression about the differences between the data being illustrated. Other graphs can be misinterpreted. In both cases, it is often the scale of the graph, which creates the problem.

Directions: Look at the graphs below. Then answer the questions and create new graphs to accurately reflect the data.

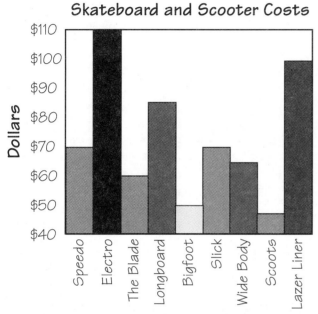

Skateboard and Scooter Costs

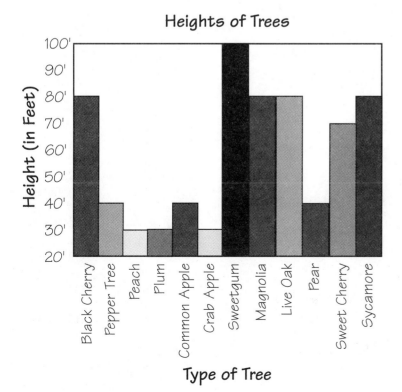

Heights of Trees

1. In looking at the graph, the Lazer Liner appears to be six times as expensive as Bigfoot. What is the actual difference in price? _____

2. Is Bigfoot twice as expensive as Scoots? _____ What is the difference in price? _____

3. Why does the Electro look more than three times as expensive as The Blade?

_____

What is the actual difference in price?

_____

4. What could be done to make the graph more accurately represent the differences between the prices of the boards and scooters? _____

5. Use a separate piece of graph paper to redesign this graph and make it reflect the real differences in prices.

6. Which three trees are 30 feet high?

_____

7. Which three trees are 40 feet high?

_____

8. Why do the trees, which are 40 feet high, seem twice as tall as the 30-foot trees? _____

9. Which four trees are 80 feet high?

_____

_____

10. Why do the 80-foot trees appear to be three times as tall as the 40-foot trees and six times as tall as the 30-foot trees? _____

11. Use a separate piece of graph paper to redesign this graph and make it reflect the real differences in heights.

Page 6

1.

Dots	0	1	2	3	4	5	6	7	8	9	10	11	12	13	14
Frequency	2	0	2	0	0	0	0	2	0	4	0	1	0	7	1

2. 23 pennies; 9 nickels;
   15 dimes;   4 quarters
   0 half dollars

Extension: Answers will vary.

Page 7

1.

	sprints	relay	long jump	sit-ups	pull-ups
6th grade boys	5	2	3	3	2
6th grade girls	4	3	3	2	1
7th grade boys	6	4	5	4	4
7th grade girls	5	6	4	3	3
8th grade boys	3	3	2	5	3
8th grade girls	4	2	2	2	2

2. 7th grade boys
3. 7th grade; The boys and girls won the most medals.
4. pull-ups; The fewest medals were awarded.
5. 54
6. 46
7.

2	3	4	5	6	7	8	9	10	11	12
1	0	1	3	4	5	3	3	2	1	1

8. 3
9. 7
10. 2, 4, 11, 12
11. 6 and 7; These combinations are the most common rolls.

Extension: Answers will vary.

Page 8

1.
2.

	Mon.	Tues.	Wed.	Thurs.	Fri.
Room 12	3	2	1	2	4
Room 13	5	3	2	3	6
Room 14	2	1	0	0	2
Room 15	3	3	1	0	1
Room 16	1	1	1	1	3
Room 17	2	0	0	3	2
Room 18	4	1	0	1	4
	20	11	5	10	22

2. 68
3. Room 14
4. Wednesday
5. Monday and Friday
6. Answers will vary.
7. 11
8. Room 13
9. 9
10. Room 12 and Room 16; There was at least one absence per day.

11.

apples	2
juice	6
colas	31
candy bar	33
chips	24
peanuts	7
raisins	3
candy jellies	35

12. candy jellies
13. apples and raisins
14. sweets
15. 141
16. $70.50

Page 10

1. 54
2. 32
3. 4
4. 15
5. 2
6. New York
7. 257
8. 281
9. There are more votes in California.
10. 13
11. Illinois and Texas; New York and Ohio
12. All states have at least 12 votes.
13. The graph can make the total of California's votes look many times greater than that of the smaller states. There is a distortion due to the scale.

Page 11

1. oxygen
2. oxygen and silicon
3. calcium and iron
4. other
5. oxygen
6. oxygen
7. 15%
8. 93%
9. Other
10. water
11. It is visual and easy to read.

Extension: Answers will vary.

Page 12

1. 3
2. 3
3. Friday
4. Carlos
5. Janet; Her work is done more regularly.
6. 16.5 hrs.
7. 17.25 hrs.
8. 2.5 hrs.

Extension: Answers will vary.

Page 14

1. 20 years
2. 40 years
3. 35 years
4. cans and bottles; 85 years
5. 7 1/2 years
6. It shows how long it takes garbage to disintegrate. Answers will vary.
7. 8 states
8. 8 states
9. 71–80%
10. 50 states
11. 61-70%
12. 81-90%
13. Answers will vary.

Page 15

1. 47% male; 53% female
2. 51% male; 49% female
3. 41% male; 59% female
4. USC and Yale
5. NYU
6. 100%; Students must be either male or female.
7. more females
8. 2nd quarter
9. 3rd quarter
10. Bulldogs 30; Wildcats 34
11. Wildcats
12. To see how his team played as the game progresses. (Answers will vary.)

Page 16

1. 30 pages
2. 50 pages
3. 65 pages
4. 70 pages
5. Wednesday
6. Monday
7. Alyssa
8. 15 pages
9. Tuesday, Friday, and Saturday
10. 410 pages
11. 300 pages
12. Alyssa
13. 90 minutes
14. 45 minutes
15. 375 minutes
16. 365 minutes
17. Catherine
18. better; She practiced more regularly.

Page 18

1. (9, 12, 14, 16, 16, 19, 22, 23, 28)
   Mode: 16
   Yes, it is in the middle and the median is the same.
   Median: 16
   Yes, it matches the mode and is close in value to most of the numbers.
2. (7, 9, 10, 10, 11, 14, 14, 15, 18, 20, 21, 31, 38)
   Mode: 10, 14
   No, the number 10 is too close to the first numbers. 14 is more representative.
   Median: 14
   No, there are many greater numbers after 14.
3. (19, 25, 28, 28, 32, 44, 48, 48, 51, 57, 64, 70)
   Mode: 28, 48
   No, 28 is too near the first numbers;

48 is more representative.
Median: 46
Yes, it's about in the middle of the values.

4. (31, 37, 39, 40, 40, 47, 47, 47, 48, 49, 49, 49, 61, 70)
Mode: 47 and 49
Yes, 47 is near the center. 49 is less representative because it is nearer to the end of the series.
Median: 47
Yes, it is representative because it is in the center and the same as one mode.

Page 19
1. Total: 6,988
Divide by: 10
Mean: 698.8 (699)
Yes, it is representative because most of the numbers are 600s and 700s.

2. Total: 65
Divide by: 9
Mean: 7.2 (7)
No, the number of moons is very variable.

3. Total: 277
Divide by: 14
Mean: 19.8 (20)
Yes, many of the numbers are near 20.

4. Total: 1,113
Divide by: 14
Mean: 79.5 (80)
Yes, it is relatively representative of the numbers; a good average.

5. Total: 2,595
Divide by: 12
Mean: 216.3 (216)
Yes, many of the numbers are in or near the low 200s.

6. Total: 112
Divide by: 16
Mean: 7
Yes, it matches the mode and is near the center between 2 and 12.

Page 20
1. Mode: 13 Median: 13
Mean: 9.6 (10)
Most representative: mode and median
Reason: They reflect the values best and are midway between high and low values.

2. Mode: 23 Median: 23
Mean: 23.3 (23)
Most representative: 23
Reason: They are all the same.

3. Mode: 8 Median: 8
Mean: 8.3 (8)
Most representative: all
Reason: They all are the same value.

4. Mode: 46 Median: 49
Mean: 51.9 (52)
Most representative: mean and median
Reason: They are closer to the center of the numbers in terms of value.

5. Mode: 23 Median: 29.5
Mean: 32.2 (32)
Most representative: median and mean
Reason: The mode is too near the first values; The others are representative of the numbers.

Page 22
1. 5 to 10 hrs.
2. 1 to 3 hrs.
3. yes
4. strong
5. positive
6. (trend line on graph)
7. yes
8. strong
9. positive
10. 12 tubs
11. 22 or more tubs

Page 23
1. 7 shots
2. 2 shots
3. yes
4. strong
5. negative
6. (trend line on graph)
7. 7 or 8 shots
8. (trend line on graph)
9. weak correlation
10. strong
11. likely

Page 24
1.
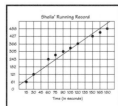
2. 122 m
3. 244 m
4. 183 m
5. strong
6. positive
7. about 503 m
8. about 533 m

Page 26
1. skateboarding
2. aerobics and biking; cheerleading and walking
3. 60
4. 16.7% (17%)
5.

Page 27
1. 8
2. It should have shown the entire scale, if possible.
3. There was not enough space.
4. no
5. no

Extension: Answers will vary.

Page 28
1. (0, 1, 3, 4, 4, 5, 5, 5, 6, 6, 6, 7, 7, 7, 7, 7, 7, 7, 8, 8, 8, 8, 8, 8, 9, 9, 9, 9, 9, 9, 9, 10, 10, 10, 10, 12)
2. 7 students
3. 1 student
4. 1 student
5. (0, 1, 12)
6. 7, 9
7. 7.5
8. 7 (7.1)
9. Yes
10. Yes. All of the measures are similar and close in value.

Extension: Answers will vary.

Page 30
1. 6
D < M R / R M   M < R D / D R
R < M D / D M

2. ABCD BACD CABD DABC
ABDC BADC CADB DACB
ACBD BCAD CBAD DBCA
ACDB BCDA CBDA DBAC
ADCB BDAC CDBA DCAB
ADBC BDCA CDAB DCBA

3. 4! = 4 x 3 x 2 x 1; 24
4. 5! = 5 x 4 x 3 x 2 x 1; 120
5. 6! = 6 x 5 x 4 x 3 x 2 x 1; 720
6. 7! = 7 x 6 x 5 x 4 x 3 x 2 x 1; 5,040
7. 10! = 10 x 9 x 8 x 7 x 6 x 5 x 4 x 3 x 2 x 1; 3,628,800

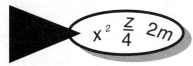

Answer Key

Page 31
1. 12 combinations
2. 10 combinations
3. 40 outfits
4. 56 combinations
5. 10 possible combinations
   vanilla + chocolate; vanilla + strawberry; vanilla + peppermint; vanilla + peach; chocolate + strawberry; chocolate + peppermint; chocolate + peach; strawberry + peppermint; strawberry + peach; peppermint + peach
6. 10 possible combinations
   vanilla + chocolate + strawberry; vanilla + chocolate + peppermint; vanilla + chocolate + peach; vanilla + strawberry + peppermint; vanilla + strawberry + peach; vanilla + peppermint + peach; chocolate + strawberry + peppermint; chocolate + strawberry + peach; chocolate + peppermint + peach; strawberry + peppermint + peach
7. 15 possible combinations
   whistle + horn; whistle + ring; whistle + balloon; whistle + gun; whistle + car; horn + ring; horn + balloon; horn + gun; horn + car; ring + balloon; ring + gun; ring + car; balloon + gun; balloon + car; gun + car

Page 32
1. H - T; 1/2
2. 1 - 2 - 3 - 4 - 5 - 6; 1/6
3. 1 - 2 - 3 - 4 - 5 - 6; 1/6
4. 1 - 2 - 3 - 4 - 5 - 6; 2/6 = 1/3
5. Red - Green - Blue - Black; 1/4
6. Red - Green - Blue - Black; 2/4 = 1/2
7. Red - Green - Blue - Black; 0
8. Red - Green - Blue - Black; 3/4
9. HH - TT - HT - TH; 2/4 = 1/2

Pages 34 and 35 Answers will vary.

Page 36
1. Possible Rolls
   6 - L1 D5 - L5 D1 - L2 D4 - L4 D2 - L3 D3
   7 - L1 D6 - L6 D1 - L2 D5 - L5 D2 - L4 D3 - L3 D4
   8 - L2 D6 - L6 D2 - L5 D3 - L3 D5 - L4 D4
   9 - L3 D6 - L6 D3 - L5 D4 - L4 - D5
   10 - L6 D4 - L4 D6 - L5 D5
   11 - L5 D6 - L6 D5
   12 - L6 D6
   Total

1	2	3	4	5	6
5	4	3	2	1	

2. 36
3. 1/36 or 2.8%
4. 2/36 = 1/18 or 5.6%
5. 4/36 = 1/9 or 11.1%
6. 6/36 = 1/6 or 16.7%
7. 4/36 = 1/9 or 11.1%
8. 1/36 or 2.8%

Page 38
1. 2/5 x 1/3 = 2/15 or 13.3%
2. 17/20 x 4/5 = 17/25 or 68%
3. 4/7 x 5/6 = 10/21 or 47.6%
4. 9/10 x 1/2 = 9/20 or 45%
5. 7/10 x 4/5 = 14/25 or 56%
6. 9/10 x 4/5 x 2/3 = 12/25 or 48%
7. 2/3 x 3/4 x 9/10 = 9/20 or 45%
8. 9/10 x 1/4 x 1/3 = 3/40 or 7.5%
9. 3/4 x 2/3 x 1/2 = 1/4 or 25%

Page 39
1. A. 1/4   B. 1/3
   C. 1/4 x 1/3 = 1/12 or 8.3%
2. A. 2/5   B. 1/4
   C. 2/5 x 1/4 = 1/10 or 10%
3. A. 2/10   B. 1/9
   C. 2/10 x 1/9 = 1/45 or 2.2%
4. A. 2/20   B. 1/19
   C. 2/20 x 1/19 = 1/190 or 0.5%
5. A. 1/8   B. 2/7
   C. 1/8 x 2/7 = 1/28 or 3.6%

Page 40
1. 13/600 or 2.2%
   10/600 or 1.7%
   23/600 or 3.8%
2. 2/600 or 0.3%
   17/600 or 2.8%
   19/600 or 3.2%
3. 1/6 or 16.7%
   2/6 or 1/3 or 33.3%
   3/6 or 1/2 or 50%
   4/6 or 2/3 or 66.6%
4. 1/12 or 8.3%
   1/12 or 1/6 or 16.7%
   3/12 or 1/4 or 25%
   5/12 or 41.7%
5. 4/52 or 1/13 or 7.7%
   8/52 or 2/13 or 15.4%
   12/52 or 3/13 or 23.1%
   16/52 or 4/13 or 30.8%
   8/52 or 2/13 or 15.4%
   32/52 or 8/13 or 61.5%

Page 41
1. 35/100 = 7/20
2. 12/100 = 3/25
3. 60/100 = 3/5
4. 45/100 = 9/20
5. 8
6. 350
7. 5,500
8. (trend line on graph)
9. weak
10. negative
11. 2.0/30 min.; 1.0/45 min.; 4.0/150 min.; 3.0/1656 min.
12. no (in this survey)

Page 42
1. 1/8 or 12.5%
2. 1/2 or 50%
3. 2/8 or 1/4 or 25%
4. 2/8 or 1/4 or 25%
5. 100%
6. 100%
7. 1/4 or 25%
8. 1/4 or 25%
9. 2/4 or 1/2 or 50%
10. 2/4 or 1/2 or 50%
11. 3/4 or 75%
12. 1/4 or 25%
13. 1/4 or 25%
14. 2/4 or 1/2 or 50%
15. 2/8 or 1/4 or 25%
16. 1/2 or 50%

Page 43 Answers will vary.

Page 44
1. 1:4 or 1 in 4
2. 3:1 or 3 to 1
3. 1:2 or 1 in 2
4. 1:1 or 50-50
5. 3:1 or 3 to 1
6. 1:3 or 1 in 3
7. 1:6 or 1 in 6
8. 5:1 or 5 to 1
9. 1:3 or 1 in 3
10. 2:1 or 2 to 1
11. 1:500 or 1 in 500
12. 499:1 or 499 to 1
13. 3:1,000,000 or 3 in 1,000,000
14. 999,997:3 or 999,997 to 3

Page 45
1. $50
2. No; $5
3. The scale starts at $40; $50
4. Start the scale at 0.
5. (student graph)
6. Peach, Plum, Crab Apple
7. Pepper Tree, Common Apple, Pear
8. The scale starts at 20' instead of 0.
9. Black Cherry, Magnolia, Live Oak, Sycamore
10. The scale is truncated (starts at 20').
11. (Graph by students.)